CHALLENGE YOUR KIDS

100 FIELD-TESTED PROBLEMS, BRAIN TEASERS, AND RIDDLES FOR SCHOOL AND HOME

VOLUME 2

DAVE VACCARO, Ed.D.

TABLE OF CONTENTS

INTRODUCTION i

Chapter One: BEGINNING PROBLEMS 1

Chapter Two: INTERMEDIATE PROBLEMS 11

Chapter Three: ADVANCED PROBLEMS................31

Chapter Four: BEGINNING HINTS AND ANSWERS 41

Chapter Five: INTERMEDIATE HINTS AND ANSWERS.....51

Chapter Six: ADVANCED HINTS AND ANSWERS................69

REFERENCES..79

ABOUT THE AUTHOR: DAVE VACCARO 83

A CUSTOMER REVIEW 83

THANK YOU..83

INTRODUCTION

Part 1 - General Information

Given the complexities of the world today, the ability to solve difficult problems is becoming increasingly more valuable. Much of our success as individuals, as well as communities, depends on the capacity to solve problems. Building this capacity in children—to consider relevant information, to reflect, and to analyze—helps to prepare them for the challenges that lie ahead.

This book provides 100 opportunities for kids to think through problems in an enjoyable way. It is intended to be used by teachers and parents with groups of children, as few as two or three or as many as thirty. It is not designed as a solo endeavor. A group setting allows them to develop the capacity to work together and to think critically, while finding the correct solution.

Although the problems may have multiple answers due to the open nature some of them possess, it is my intent to have your children burrow down to the one correct answer that I have provided. The process of digging down is the important work to help your kids develop the capacity to think. Almost all of these problems are based on real life. While a few are theoretical, they are still worthy of consideration. The journey of figuring out the answer is much more important than the actual answer itself because it builds both an awareness of their own abilities as well as the value of solving problems with others, a process no doubt they will repeat many times in life.

Part 2 - Field-Testing with Elementary and Middle School Kids

Several months before I published this book, I visited two local elementary schools and one middle school to field-test these problems. The students rated my problems on how well they enjoyed each problem using a 1 - 5 point scale with 5 being the highest rating. Only problems that scored an average of three or higher were included in this book.

The students also determined the level of difficulty for each problem using the following terms: easy, medium, or hard. Again, I used their consensus rating to identify the level of difficulty for each problem included in this book. So, I am confident that these problems work with kids.

Part 3 - Revised Bloom's Taxonomy Labeling

To assist teachers, I have labeled each problem/question with my approximation of the Revised Bloom's Taxonomy Level. This is "only" an approximation of the level of difficulty for each problem and question. I acknowledge that some teachers and some parents may see a specific problem/question belonging to a different level of difficulty than the one I assigned. I understand and respect their opinions.

The six levels in ascending order of difficulty are as follows: Remembering, Understanding, Applying, Analyzing, Evaluating, and Creating.

REVISED BLOOM'S TAXONOMY

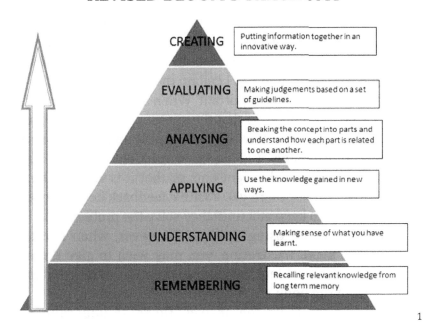

CREATING	Putting information together in an innovative way.
EVALUATING	Making judgements based on a set of guidelines.
ANALYSING	Breaking the concept into parts and understand how each part is related to one another.
APPLYING	Use the knowledge gained in new ways.
UNDERSTANDING	Making sense of what you have learnt.
REMEMBERING	Recalling relevant knowledge from long term memory

1

Note 1: The title, REVISED BLOOM'S TAXONOMY, is not part of the original image above.

Note 2: In the figure above, the image uses the British spelling for ANALYSING not the American spelling which is ANALYZING.

HOW TO USE THIS BOOK EFFECTIVELY

After creating these problems, I went into elementary and middle school classrooms to test the problems with students. The best 100 were compiled and appear in this book. Virtually every time I have had great success, and the children say, "Give us another problem!"

The book is organized into three levels based on student evaluation: beginning, intermediate, and advanced. These labels are an approximation because what may be easy for one kid may be difficult for another. You will have to decide what is appropriate for your kids.

100 Field-Tested Problems, Brain Teasers, and Riddles for School and Home

Chapter One

BEGINNING PROBLEMS

1. 3x3 Square

[Analyzing]

Look at the figure below.

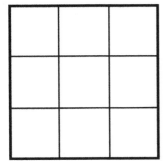

Question: How many possible squares are in this figure?

The hint and answer are on page 41.

2. A Coded Message

[Applying]

Coded messages have been used for centuries. In wartime, spies have used them to avoid capture and detection. You can use coded messages to keep your own ideas private from outside detection.

Question: Can you decode the following message consisting of four words?

9-14 / 7-15-4 / 23-5 / 20-18-21-19-20

The hint and answer are on page 41.

3. A Small Pond

[Understanding]

One sunny day, Kamran looked at his own reflection in a small pond of water. At first, his reflection seemed to be quite ordinary. However, when looking again he could hardly believe what he saw. It reminded him of his religious studies when he was a child in elementary school.

Question: What did he see in his reflection that amazed him?

The hint and answer are on page 42.

The hint and answer are on page 42.

4. Finding Values

[Applying]

$x + x = 15$

$y + y + y = 36$

$x + y + z = 119.5$

Question: What are the values of x, y, and z?

The hint and answer are on page 42.

5. The Bathing Cap

[Applying]

I saw it, but I still don't believe it. Swimmers took a bathing cap into the water to test how far it could be stretched. By swinging it underwater back and forth, the bathing cap continued to expand.[2]

Question: Can you finish this sentence? The bathing cap got so large that a female swimmer was able to_____.

The hint and answer are on page 42.

6. Solve Me

[Understanding]

Look at the tiles below.

ESS	D	ER	AM	BL	GO	CA	I

Question: Can you rearrange these tiles in order to solve the message?

The hint and answer are on page 43.

7. The Effects of Space

[Evaluating]

Being in space on the International Space Station is the experience of a lifetime. Weightlessness is amazing. One astronaut spent 15 months there while his identical twin, also an astronaut, remained on earth. When he returned from space, the scientists concluded that the noticeable change in him could be attributed to the effects of space.[3]

Question: What did the scientists conclude about the effects of space?

The hint and answer are on page 43.

8. A Better Way

[Analyzing]

A wealthy married man lived in a home next to his elderly parents. He wanted to be able to personally visit them daily to check on their well-being. A simple phone call would not suffice. The problem was that there was so much snowy, inclement weather that the 50-yard trek to their home each day was a nuisance. So, he constructed another way to go to their home.

Question: What new way did he construct to visit is parents?

The hint and answer are on page 43.

9. Dice Rolls

When rolling one die the number of possible combinations is six (1, 2, 3, 4, 5, 6). As more dice are used, more combinations become possible beyond the initial six combinations with one die.[4]

Questions:
1. How many combinations are possible with 2 dice?
2. How many combinations are possible with 3 dice?
3. How many combinations are possible with 4 dice?

The hint and answers are on page 44.

10. Tigers

[Analyzing]

Tigers have stripes that help them blend into their surroundings, but their bright orange color is a dead giveaway to us. Yet, these animals are excellent hunters.

Question: If their bright orange color is so obvious to us, how is it possible for tigers to sneak up on their prey?

The hint and answer are on page 44.

11. Fireflies

[Analyzing]

At the end of spring every year, synchronous fireflies (*Photinus carolinus*) put on a two-week light show in the Great Smoky Mountains National Park as they start and stop flashing in unison. The National Park Service reports that this is the only species in the United States that synchronizes its "flashing light patterns."[5]

Question: What is the reason for these synchronized light patterns?

The hint and answer are on page 44.

12. The Project

[Analyzing]

After watching the evening news in 1960, Jim gave his teenage son Dave a unique project that would last for many weeks at their Florida home. The tools Jim provided his son consisted of a shovel and a wheelbarrow. For several weeks, Dave worked diligently. When the project was about halfway complete, his father told him that he had changed his mind. The son was now charged with putting the area back into its original condition.

Question: What was the unfinished project given to the son?

The hint and answer are on page 45.

13. Rebus Writing

[Applying]

Rebus writing uses pictures and sometimes parts of words to represents words or phrases.

Rebuses can be found in recent as well as ancient literature.[6]

TO   TO

7

Question: Can you read the sentence above?

The hint and answer are on page 45.

14. Improvise

[Applying]

Stephanie was about to begin a presentation when she realized the microphone was not working. There was no time to get another one. Because she wanted the small audience to hear a special recording from her iPhone, she came up with an ingenious solution.

Question: What was it?

The hint and answer are on page 45.

15. Political Office

[Remembering]

George H. W. Bush, Al Gore, and Dan Quayle are well known American citizens. They have all served in the same political office.

Question: Which political office did they have in common?

The hint and answer are on page 46.

16. I Refused

[Remembering]

On December 1, 1955, a black woman sat in her seat on the bus after her long day of work. When a white man boarded the bus, all the seats in the white section were taken. So, the white bus driver told her and others to stand up. She refused and soon after she was arrested.[8]

Question: What was her name?

The hint and answer are on page 46.

17. What Is Making That Noise?

[Understanding]

A man kept hearing a clawing noise from the gutter on his home. He thought it was a bird looking for bugs. When he went outside in the cold to scare it away, there were no birds.

Question: What was making that noise?

The hint and answer are on page 46.

18. What Am I?

[Understanding]

I travel around the world, but I stay in one spot.

Question: What am I?

The hint and answer are on page 47.

19. Adding to the Confusion

[Applying]

John, Jim, and Joe were identical triplets. This only occurs once in 200 million births. You really could not tell them apart from one another, and their mother would often call them by the wrong name. It was confusing. When all three men got married, it didn't get any better.

Question: Why didn't it get better?

The hint and answer are on page 47.

20. A Rectangle

[Applying]

3 ft.

6 ft.

Questions: What is the perimeter of this rectangle? What is the area of this rectangle?

The hint and answers are on page 47.

21. Are You Afraid of Me?

[Understanding]

You should be afraid of me. I can rattle you and your belongings, and I can do much, much worse. Consider yourself lucky if I never visit your town.

Question: Who am I?

The hint and answer are on page 48.

22. Bucket of Water

[Applying]

Keira claimed that she could turn a bucket of water upside down without any water falling out. Her friends doubted her. As it turns out, Keira was right when she demonstrated this feat to a group of her friends.

Question: How did Keira do it?

The hint and answer are on page 48.

23. A Cube

[Applying]

2 inches

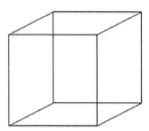

Question: What is the surface area of this cube?

The hint and answer are on page 48.

24. My Birthday

[Understanding]

One of our nice traditions is the celebration of one's birthday. This is a special day that is usually accompanied by cards and presents. However, I know of a woman who is 20 years old, but she has only had six birthdays.

Question: How is this possible?

The hint and answer are on page 49.

25. Brightly Colored

[Remembering]

Dart frogs are common to both Central and South America. These small frogs are brightly colored. Some people claim they are very beautiful, while others are not so sure.

Question: Why are these dart frogs so brightly colored?

The hint and answer are on page 49.

26. Who Is Knocking on My Window?

[Analyzing]

A man in Ireland reported that a seagull had been knocking on his home window every day for two years. And the seagull would not go away until the man did one specific thing.[9]

Question: What did the man do to get the seagull to stop knocking on his window for the rest of the day?

The hint and answer are on page 49.

Chapter Two

INTERMEDIATE PROBLEMS

27. Another Rebus Writing

[Applying]

Rebus writing uses pictures and sometimes parts of words to represents words or phrases.

M   +

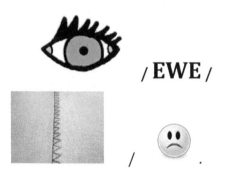

/ **EWE** /

/

Question: Can you read the four-word sentence above?

The hint and answer are on page 51.

28. Table Tennis

[Analyzing]

Margie played in a double-elimination table tennis tournament. She was the eventual grand champion even though she had one loss. There were 16 players entered in this tournament.

Question: How many total games were played in the tournament?

The hint and answer are on page 51.

29. Mental Division 1

[Applying]

Divide these numbers in your head.

1. Divide 800 by 2 in your head seven times.

2. Divide 800 by 2 in your head eight times.

Questions: What is the answer to #1? What is the answer to #2?

The hint and answers are on page 52.

30. Running on Water

[Analyzing]

We were invited out to our friend's lake house for the weekend. While walking along her property the next day, I saw something I couldn't believe. So, I looked again and saw Bahiyyih, a nine-year-old girl, running on water. She probably ran 30 or 40 feet before she went under the water. This is impossible, yet I saw her do it.

Question: Can you explain this mystery?

The hint and answer are on page 52.

31. The Document

[Applying]

Look at the letters below.

T T S N O N I O C I U T

Question: Can you unscramble these letters to form the right word?

The hint and answer are on page 52.

32. The Walking Stick

[Analyzing]

Jace purchased a walking stick for $20. When out on the trail, he continually strikes the ground while walking in the woods. There is a reason why he does this.

Question: Why does he do this?

The hint and answer are on page 53.

33. Dimes and Cups

[Analyzing]

There are 3 plastic cups and 8 dimes on a table. Put the dimes in the cups in such a manner so the following conditions are present: (1) there is no empty cup; and (2) there must be five dimes in one cup and three dimes in another cup.

Question: Can this be done? If so, how?

The hint and answer are on page 53.

34. Strange Rescuer

[Analyzing]

A man went fishing in his boat on a local river. Unfortunately, he fell out of his boat into the turbulent water. He swam against the swift current as best he could until an unlikely rescuer saved him.[10]

Question: Who was the unlikely rescuer?

The hint and answer are on page 53.

35. One Die

[Applying]

When rolling one die, the probability of rolling a six are 1/6. Now add one more die and roll them.

Question: What is the probability of rolling a six combination using a pair of dice?

The hint and answer are on page 54.

36. Lights During the Day

[Analyzing]

Alexandra and her children were out in her front yard on a sunny day. They were enjoying a game of hide-and-seek when gradually the mailbox post lights came on. It was 3 p.m. in the early afternoon, but normally they do not come on until darkness settles in.

Question: Seeing your street lights come on in the early afternoon is unusual, what could explain this?

The hint and answer are on page 54.

37. Unscramble

[Applying]

Look at the letters below.

O F A S F D D L I O R E

Question: Can you unscramble these letters to form an 8-letter word and a 4-letter word?

The hint and answer are on page 54.

38. Mount Rushmore

[Remembering]

Mount Rushmore has four presidents' faces carved into its granite surface. George Washington represents the struggle for independence. Thomas Jefferson represents the idea of government by the people. Theodore Roosevelt represents the role of the United States in world affairs.[11]

Questions: Who is the fourth president? What two things does he represent?

The hint and answers are on page 55.

39. Rearrange the Tiles

[Understanding]

Look at the tiles below.

T	A	TISH	HE	ING	RE	BRI	COM

Question: Can you rearrange these tiles in order to figure out this quotation?

The hint and answer are on page 55.

40. A Long Way Home

[Analyzing]

This is a true story. An owner lost his dog, and quite some time later it was found 2,000 miles away. Unfortunately, the owner was unable to go and retrieve his dog. Someone came up with a brilliant plan to reunite the dog with its owner.[12]

Question: What was the plan?

The hint and answer are on page 55.

41. Mental Division 2

[Applying]

1. Divide 10,000 by 5 in your head four times.

2. Divide 10,000 by 5 in your head five times.

Questions: What is the answer to (1)? What is the answer to (2)?

The hint and answers are on page 56.

42. Several Operators

[Remembering]

The process started in one location and ended many miles away. It involved several operators with several horses. The official process was only used for 18 months beginning in 1860 and ending in 1861. This process is something we take for granted today.[13]

Questions: What was this process called? What did they do?

The hint and answers are on page 56.

43. Not So Common Word

[Applying]

Put the following letters in the correct order to form a word.

O	E	Z	Y	K	N

[14]

Question: What does this term mean?

The hint and answer are on page 56.

44. Trapped by Fire

[Evaluating]

A married couple lived in a really nice neighborhood in the western part of the United States. One afternoon, they found themselves encircled by a raging forest fire. They could not get to their car to escape, nor could they stay in the house which was engulfed by flames. It seemed like they would not survive, but then they looked around and came up with a clever solution to this disaster.[15]

Question: What was the clever solution?

The hint and answer are on page 57.

45. Roman Numerals

[Applying]

Look at the Roman numeral below.

MDCCCLXV

Questions: What is this number? If this number were a date, what is its significance?

The hint and answers are on page 57.

46. Goats on a Dam Wall

[Evaluating]

The bare and almost vertical wall of the Cingno Dam in Italy does not prevent Ibex goats from climbing it. As many as 20 goats can be seen at one time on the dam wall, which is more than 120 feet tall. At the top of the wall, the pitch is almost 85 degrees. Strangely, it is only the female goats and their young that climb the wall.[16]

Questions:
1. What causes these goats to scale a nearly vertical dam wall?
2. Why is it only the female goats and their young that climb the wall?

The hint and answers are on page 57.

47. Leslie's Goal

[Applying]

Leslie's goal is to hike exactly 20 miles at her week-long vacation at Cumberland Mountain State Park. She wants to hike all six trails at least once, but no trail more than three times.

Question: What exact combination of trails should she select from the following list to achieve her goal given the trail lengths listed below?

Red = 1.0 mi.
Yellow = 2.1 mi.
Blue = 6.0 mi.
Orange = 0.7 mi.
White = 2.0 mi.
Green = 3.0 mi.

The hint and answer are on page 58.

48. Is There Water on the Moon?

[Evaluating]

Scientists have wondered for many years if there was water on the moon. Some scientists have thought so while others have not. Looking up at night we see our closest celestial body and wonder.[17]

Questions: Does water exist on the moon? If so, what form is it and where is it located?

The hint and answers are on page 58.

49. Tennessee Road Trip

[Understanding]

Leaving Chattanooga at 2 p.m., Wyatt drove for two hours without stopping and arrived in Franklin at 3 p.m.

Question: If this was a two-hour car trip, what happened to the missing hour?

The hint and answer are on page 58.

50. Hard-Boiled Eggs

[Analyzing]

When Jeanne moved into her new mountain home, she was very happy. It had been a dream that was a long time coming. After a week passed, Jeanne decided to boil some eggs for breakfast. Usually they boiled in about 12 minutes, but when she peeled one it was not done. She estimated it would take a few more minutes to get the eggs hard boiled.[18]

Question: Why was it taking longer to hard boil eggs in Jeanne's new home?

The hint and answer are on page 59.

51. Fresh Water

[Applying]

After wrecking your boat, you become stranded on an island in the Atlantic Ocean. You find no fresh water on this small island. You only have a few items with you. Some of them include: a large bowl, a cup, a clear piece of saran wrap, and a first aid kit.

Question: Using just these items, how can you make fresh water?

The hint and answer are on page 59.

52. A Raisin

[Remembering]

If you put a raisin in a glass of water, you will see it expand beyond its original shape. This can occur with other dehydrated fruits as well.

Question: What is this process called?

The hint and answer are on page 59.

53. Long Distance Runner

[Understanding]

Grace was a fine athlete from Middle Tennessee who competed in many long-distance runs in her home state. Usually, she came in first or second in these contests. However, that was not the case in her most recent competition against East Tennessee athletes at Clingmans Dome in the Great Smoky Mountains National Park. To her dismay, Grace finished eleventh.

Question: Why did Grace finish eleventh instead of her usual first or second?

The hint and answer are on page 60.

54. Turning Left

[Understanding]

A man leaves home and turns left three times, only to return home facing two men wearing masks.

Question: Who are the two men?

The hint and answer are on page 60.

55. Partners

[Understanding]

We are partners and we work well. Separately we accomplish little, but together we can locate any point on the earth.

Question: Who are we?

The hint and answer are on page 60.

56. Two Oval Shapes

[Analyzing]

While opening his bathroom door, a man sees two small oval shapes on the linen closet door inside of his bathroom. Since this is a wooden door, he thought the oval shapes might have been defections in the wood, but they were not. As he observed it over the next week, he noticed that they would appear at certain times and then disappear.

Question: Can you determine what these shapes were and how they got there?

The hint and answer are on page 61.

57. How Many Package Deals?

[Applying]

Jordan power washes condominium driveways for $137.50 each, and then he cleans the outside condominium windows for $55. This is a package deal. His goal is to earn a minimum of $2,000 this week.

Question: What is the minimum number of complete condo home packages he needs to sell to reach his goal?

The hint and answer are on page 61.

58. Stay Alive

[Evaluating]

If your car breaks down in freezing winter weather in an isolated area and you become stranded, stay calm and stay warm. You know that your car engine starts, but the car will not move forward or backward. Experts recommend that you stay hydrated but not eat snow.

Questions: Why should you not eat snow? How can you get water?

The hint and answers are on page 61.

59. Eight Years

[Applying]

There are 365 days in a normal calendar year.

Question:

How many days are there in the following eight years: 2017, 2018, 2019, 2020, 2021, 2022, 2023, and 2024?

The hint and answer are on page 62.

60. Hold Your Horses

[Understanding]

As humans, we tend to believe because we can visualize, think, and speak that we have a monopoly on intelligence. However, other species have intelligence as well. Take dolphins for example. It has been documented that dolphins communicate with one another through a myriad of sounds. Elephants appear to mourn their dead. And scientists have recently discovered that horses can recognize and remember things.[19]

Question: What recent factor did scientists discover about a horse's memory and recognition?

The hint and answer are on page 62.

61. More Than 2,000 Miles

[Remembering]

I am over 2,000 miles long and cross through 14 states. I have been in existence since 1937. It is estimated that around two million people visit me each year.

Question: Who am I?

The hint and answer are on page 62.

62. Unusual Villages

[Analyzing]

Vietnamese refugees living in Cambodia have created unusual villages that require no immigration papers. These detached villages operate like other Cambodian villages since they have schools, stores, barbers, and places to play soccer. When you first look at them you immediately know how unusual they really are.[20]

Question: What is so unusual about these villages?

The hint and answer are on page 63.

63. Gasoline

[Applying]

A gallon of gasoline costs $2.55 at the local market. I can travel 245.7 miles using 12.6 gallons of gasoline.

Questions: How much does it cost me to buy 12.6 gallons? What is the average number of miles per gallon I can drive?

The hint and answers are on page 63.

64. Near the Continental Divide

[Remembering]

I have something in common with some women, my name is one of them. I have long, cold, and moderately snowy winters. I am the state capital, but before that I was a gold camp during the Gold Rush period. I am located in Lewis and Clark County. My state has the largest migratory elk population in the United States. I am near the Continental Divide.

Questions: What is my name? What is the name of my state?

The hint and answers are on page 63.

65. Six Questions

[Applying]

There are 60 seconds in a minute, 60 minutes in an hour, and 24 hours in a day. There are 7 days in a week and 52 weeks and one day in a year except leap year. And there are 12 months in a year.

Questions:
1. How many months are there in three years of 2017, 2018, and 2019?
2. How many weeks are there in the same three years?
3. How many days are there in same three years?
4. How many hours are there in same three years?
5. How may minutes are there in same three years?
6. How many seconds are there in same three years?

The hint and answers are on page 64.

66. Improving Indoor Air Quality

[Analyzing]

Many people living in industrialized nations spend much of their lives indoors. It makes sense to focus on improving indoor air quality in a cost-effective and sustainable manner. There are several components that could accomplish this goal. One component is to use the integration of smart-sensor-controlled air cleaning technologies. Another component is to use non-toxic products.[21]

Question: Can you name a natural component to improve air quality?

The hint and answer are on page 64.

67. A Circle

[Applying]

In the circle below, "r" = 4 inches.

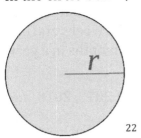

Questions: What is the circumference of this circle? What is the area?

The hint and answers are on page 64.

68. Small, but Powerful

[Remembering]

I am small, but I can do damage. Cars are usually my victims. When I come to your town you won't greet me with the "key" to your city. That is for sure. However, you can relax because I don't usually stay very long in any one location. I've got to be moving on.

Question: Who am I?

The hint and answer are on page 65.

69. Bigger Than Two States

[Remembering]

Though I am not a state, I am larger than Rhode Island and Delaware combined. I was the first of my kind and I have been around since 1872. My largest lake is more than 131 square miles, and my highest peak is 11,358 feet. Between 3 and 4 million people visit me annually.

Question: Who am I?

The hint and answer are on page 65.

70. Riptides

[Analyzing]

Ocean riptides are very dangerous. A man who was an average swimmer got caught in one and was pulled out to sea. At first he couldn't free himself, but fortunately by remaining calm he realized three things he needed to do. When he did them, he was able to free himself and swim to shore.[23]

Question: What were the three things?

The hint and answers are on page 65.

71. Work for Free

[Understanding]

I work for free. I have no health insurance, nor a 401K plan, but I am not complaining. That's just the way it is for me. I work efficiently and get all my assigned tasks done, usually on time.

Question: Who am I?

The hint and answer are on page 66.

72. Window Shopping

[Analyzing]

A woman walked by a storefront and could not believe her eyes. A man was stuck to the outside glass of a storefront window with his feet off the ground. She saw his face, hands, and feet while the rest of him was covered in black garbage bags and gray duct tape.[24]

Question: Can you explain this to me?

The hint and answer are on page 66.

73. No Train Engines

[Remembering]

I have passengers and cargo. I have stations and depots. I have conductors and stockholders, but I have no train engines.

Question: Who am I?

The hint and answer are on page 66.

74. Methane Gas

[Analyzing]

While the majority of greenhouse gases come from carbon dioxide (about 82%), methane gas is 20 times more potent than carbon dioxide. One polluting sector that is often overlooked is agriculture and farming.[25]

Questions: What is a major producer of methane on a farm? In what three forms does it release methane?

The hint and answers are on page 67.

75. Coded Message 2

[Applying]

Coded messages have been used for centuries. In times of war, spies used coded messages to avoid capture and detection. You can use coded messages to protect your own ideas from outside detection.

Question: Can you decode the following four-word phase?

19-7-4 / 3-4-2-11-0-17-0-19-8-14-13 / 14-5 / 8-13-3-4-15-4-13-3-4-13-2-4

The hint and answer are on page 67.

76. Find the Answer

[Applying]

Here is a fun activity. Give it a try.

1. Write the number of the month in which you were born.
2. Multiply it by 4.
3. Add 13.
4. Multiply by 100.
5. Divide by 4.
6. Subtract 200.
7. Add the day of the month you were born.
8. Multiply by 2.
9. Subtract 40.
10. Multiply by 50.
11. Take the last two digits of the year you were born and add them to the total so far.
12. Subtract 10,500.

Question: What is the answer?

The hint and answer are on page 67.

Chapter Three

ADVANCED PROBLEMS

77. Tiles

[Understanding]

Look at the tiles below.

T	T	N	E	I	C	I	S	S	S

Question: Can you rearrange these tiles in the correct order to form the word?

The hint and answer are on page 69.

78. Tiger Attacks

[Evaluating]

In one part of India near Bangladesh, 50-60 people a year were killed by tigers. This terrorized the local residents. Finally, someone came up with a solution to this problem, and the death toll there dropped dramatically. Unfortunately, this only lasted for a limited time, and then the tiger attacks resumed.

Question: Even though the solution was not permanent, what did the people do to stop the tiger-related deaths?

The hint and answer are on page 69.

79. A Football

I am known as a football, but you do not throw me or catch me. You will not see me on game day or even at a practice, yet I am still very important. Only a few have ever carried me.

Question: Who am I?

The hint and answer are on page 69.

80. Four-Wheeler

[Analyzing]

Two friends ran their four-wheeler down a muddy road after a day of cutting firewood. Unfortunately, they ran off the side of the road near a culvert, and one wheel dropped into a ditch below the road level.

Question: How did they get the four-wheeler out of the ditch?

The hint and answer are on page 70.

81. Container Ships

[Analyzing]

Container ships are now among the largest seafaring vessels. They carry hundreds of metal containers filled with products from all over the world. When loading a container ship, it is important to avoid overloading as that could lead to the ship sinking.[26]

Question: What do dock workers do to avoid overloading a container ship for summertime seawater?

The hint and answer are on page 70.

82. Surviving an Avalanche

[Evaluating]

If you get caught in an avalanche and become buried under the snow, there are four things you can do to stay alive. They are: (1) hold one arm straight above your head in the direction of the snow's surface. It is easy to become disoriented as to which way is up. By spitting out a small amount of saliva you will know as saliva will run downwards; (2) Dig an air pocket around your nose and face. This should give you 30 minutes of breathing time before others can dig you out. Take a deep breath and hold it for a few seconds, which will give you some breathing room.[27]

Question: What are steps three and four?

The hint and answers are on page 70.

83. Rainbow-Colored Lights

[Analyzing]

They shot up like pillars in the cold Wyoming night sky. We could not get over the rainbow-colored lights peering through the fog in our little town of Pinedale.[28]

Question: What accounted for the rainbow-colored lights?

The hint and answer are on page 71.

84. A Misunderstanding

[Analyzing]

In 1968, on an early, wet morning, an ironworker drove up Federal Highway to his mall job site north of Fort Lauderdale. He parked his car and went to work tying metal rods. At the end of the day, he returned to his car to see that the engine hood was up. Someone had disconnected his car battery. He thought someone must have been trying to steal the battery, but took off when he was discovered. The ironworker was wrong.

Question: What really happened here?

The hint and answer are on page 71.

85. Adjusting a Spotlight

[Creating]

A tall woman wanted to adjust a center spotlight at the end of her boat dock. Her boat slip was 8 feet wide so, she needed a 2x12 board at least 10 feet long to stand on in order to span the opening. She looked at all of her boards in her wood pile, but none were 10 feet long. The lumber yard was more than a 45-minute drive, and she had no interest in driving there. She thought for a moment and then came up with the perfect solution.

Question: What was the solution?

The hint and answer are on page 71.

86. I Created Many Things

[Analyzing]

George Washington Carver, born in 1865, worked with peanuts, sweet potatoes, and soybeans to create many new products. He also developed crop rotations with a special emphasis on the nitrogen replenishing role of legume products.[29]

Questions:
1. He made wood shavings into what new product?
2. He made cotton into what new product?

The hint and answers are on page 72.

87. Safer Water

[Evaluating]

Randy went camping in the wilderness for a few days to reconnect with nature. After two days passed, his water supply had become depleted, and he was unable to build a fire. Even though there was a stream nearby, he was afraid to drink water directly from it. So, he decided to find a safer way to get a drink.[30]

Question: What was this safer way?

The hint and answer are on page 72.

88. Fifty States

[Applying]

There are 50 states and a several territories that makeup the United States of America. Some states are known for hospitality while others are known for having industrialized centers. However, one state has done something quite unique. Hawaii passed an unusual law that grew out of necessity.[31]

Questions: What unusual law did Hawaii enact? Why did the state pass it?

The hint and answers are on page 72.

89. No Keys

[Understanding]

I have locks but no keys. I am considered to be a time-saver by many people, and I have been around since 1914. If you saw a picture of me, you would probably know what I am.

Question: What am I?

The hint and answer are on page 73.

90. Setting A Record

[Remembering]

On October 14, 1947, Chuck Yeager flew his Bell X-1 at Mach 1 speed. He flew his aircraft at an altitude of 45,000 feet.

Question: What record did he set on that day?

The hint and answer are on page 73.

91. Cryogenic Freezing

[Analyzing]

Is cryogenic freezing possible? Believe it or not, scientists have brought back to life one animal species that has been frozen for 40,000 years.[32]

Question: What animal did they bring back to life?

The hint and answer are on page 73.

92. The Color of Snow

[Analyzing]

For most of my life, I thought snow was always white, but according to several news reports Russia has experienced orange snow. This is not a joke. Some parts of Russia have really had orange snow.[33]

Question: How was this possible?

The hint and answer are on page 74.

93. We Made a Big Difference

[Remembering]

We helped win World War II by transmitting tactical messages that our enemies could not decipher. There were approximately 350 of us who learned this special language while serving in the United States Marine Corps. At Iwo Jima, we passed over 800 error-free messages in a 48-hour period.[34]

Question: Who were we?

The hint and answer are on page 74.

94. Getting Out of Quicksand

[Analyzing]

Getting out of shallow quicksand requires four precise steps. The good news is that most quicksand pits are only a couple of feet deep. Here are the first two steps: (1) drop everything that you are carrying to make yourself lighter and more buoyant, and try to get out of your shoes; and (2) upon first entering the quicksand, take a few quick steps backwards before the quicksand has a chance to take hold.[35]

Question: What are steps three and four?

The hint and answers are on page 74.

95. A Dakota Fire Pit

[Analyzing]

A Dakota fire pit is also known as a Dakota fire hole. It is constructed first by digging a hole in the ground one foot deep and one foot wide. Then, the bottom of the hole is enlarged to handle larger pieces of wood. About a foot away, a six-inch-wide tunnel is dug from the ground surface, angling towards the bottom of the fire pit. As the fire burns air is sucked into the tunnel, which keeps the fire burning.[36]

Question: A Dakota fire pit has three distinct advantages over a normal fire pit. What are the three distinct advantages?

The hint and answers are on page 75.

96. Paint Purchase

[Applying]

Joe has a contract to paint the bedroom walls in 10 identical apartments. Each apartment has three rectangular bedrooms. Each bedroom has one door and one window. The doors and windows are not being painted. Below are the dimensions of the apartments:

- Bedroom one measures 10 ft. by 12 ft.
- Bedroom two measures 12 ft. by 14 ft.
- Bedroom three measures 14 ft. by 16 ft.
- The wall height in each bedroom is 8 ft.
- Each bedroom door is 3 ft. by 7 ft. and each bedroom window is 6 ft. by 6 ft.

Question: If a gallon of latex wall paint covers 400 square feet, how many gallons will Joe have to buy to paint all of the bedroom walls, but not the bedroom doors and windows?

The hint and answer are on page 75.

97. A Big Appetite

[Analyzing]

I have a big appetite. Whenever I open my trap nothing nearby escapes me. The amount I can consume is huge, and I take my time about it. Doing this relieves my depression. I do not intend to be rushed. After I do finish, it may be quite a while before my appetite kicks in again. I have been called a cenote and a doline, but that doesn't bother me.

Question: What am I?

The hint and answer are on page 76.

98. The Bottle

[Applying]

Two campers were out in the desert on a three-day adventure with no food or water. They went there with no tools or knives. One of them found a long neck glass root beer bottle. He wanted to knock out the bottom while still being able to use the bottle to scoop up water. The only thing he had with him that might help him was a large nail.[37]

Question: How did he knock out the bottom of the bottle without otherwise damaging it?

The hint and answer are on page 76.

99. Boiling River

[Analyzing]

Deep in the Amazon there is a four-mile-long river that kills. The Shanay-Timpishka gets as hot as 196 degrees Fahrenheit, and it boils anything that dares enter into it alive. For a river to get this hot, it must be near an active volcano. However, the closest volcano is more than 400 miles away. Dr. Andres Ruzo believes he knows the heat source.[38]

Question: What is this heat source of the Boiling River?

The hint and answer are on page 76.

100. Big Square

[Analyzing]

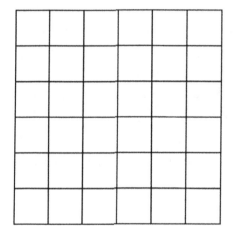

Question: Look at the figure above. How many possible squares are there? Look carefully. Write down your answer and do not share it with anyone.

The hint and answer are on page 77.

Chapter Four

BEGINNING
HINTS AND ANSWERS

1. 3x3 Square

Hint: Some squares may overlap.

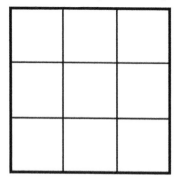

Answer: (1) large 3x3 square + (9) single squares + (4) 2x2 squares = 14 squares.

2. A Coded Message

Hint: Money.

Answer: In God We Trust.

3. A Small Pond

Hint: Angels have them.

Answer: He saw a halo.

4. Finding Values

Hint: 7.5

Answers:

$x = 7.5$

$y = 12$

$z = 100$

5. The Bathing Cap

Hint: Park.

Answer: "sit inside it."

Note: The bathing cap stretched so large that the swimmer could sit inside of it.

6. Solve Me

Hint: Patriotic song.

Answer: God Bless America.

7. The Effects of Space

Hint: Higher.

Answer: Space makes you taller. Scott was now 2 inches taller than his twin brother Mark after his 15 months on the space station.

Note: On earth gravity compresses your spinal disks, but not so in space. Therefore, Scott's spinal column actually lengthened.

8. A Better Way

Hint: Channel.

Answer: He had a tunnel built between the two homes. It was big enough to drive a golf cart through.

9. Dice Rolls

Hint: Squared.

Answers:

1. 36

2. 216

3. 1,296

10. Tigers

Hint: Animal vision.

Answer: Most animals can't distinguish between different colors, so the animals don't really see the tiger.

11. Fireflies

Hint: Ritual.

Answer: Their light patterns are part of their mating display. The males fly around and flash while the stationary females respond with a flash in return.

12. The Project

Hint: Threat of conflict.

Answer: His dad had him dig a bomb shelter during the Cuban Missile Crisis.

13. Rebus Writing

Hint: Shakespeare.

Answer: To be, or not to be? This is a famous line from Shakespeare's play, Hamlet.

14. Improvise

Hint: Container.

Answer: She put the iPhone in a wide mouth drinking glass that helped to amplify the sound.

15. Political Office

Hint: Votes only to break a tie.

Answer: They all served as vice president of the United States.

16. I Refused

Hint: Her first name is similar to a common flower and her last name is similar to playgrounds.

Answer: Her name was Rosa Parks.

17. What Is Making That Noise?

Hint: Cold outside.

Answer: Ice was melting and slipping inside of the metal downspout.

18. What Am I?

Hints: Sticky. You have used me before.

Answer: I am a stamp.

19. Adding to the Confusion

Hint: Their marriages.

Answer: They married three identical female triplets.

20. A Rectangle

Hint: Add and multiply.

Answers:

P = 2 lengths + 2 widths = 18 ft.

A = l x w = 18 sq. ft.

21. Are You Afraid of Me?

Hint: Shake.

Answer: I am an earthquake.

22. Bucket of Water

Hint: Force.

Answer: She quickly swung a bucket of water with her arm in a circle above her head. Centripetal force kept the water inside the bucket.

23. A Cube

Hint: Multiply.

Answer: Surface area = $6 \times s^2 = 6 \times (2 \times 2) = 24$ sq. inches

24. My Birthday

Hint: When was she born?

Answer: She was born on February 29th.

Note: This date occurs only once in a four-year period. Some example years include 2000, 2004, and 2008.

25. Brightly Colored

Hint: A warning.

Answer: They are highly poisonous. Their bright colors are a warning to stay away.

26. Who Is Knocking on My Window?

Hint: Something we all like.

Answer: He feeds the seagull.

Chapter Five

INTERMEDIATE HINTS AND ANSWERS

27. Another Rebus Writing

Hint: My.

Answer: My you seem sad.

28. Table Tennis

Hint: Each player can lose twice before being eliminated. Margie has lost once, but is the winner of the losing bracket.

Answer: 31 games is the answer.

Note: Margie is the winner of the losing bracket and has lost once. Then, she plays the winner of the winning bracket and wins. That would be the 30th game, but they must play again because it is double elimination. This makes it the 31st game.

29. Mental Division 1

Hint: Mixed numeral.

Answers:

1. 6 and 1/4 or 6.25.
2. 3 and 1/8 or 3.125.

30. Running on Water

Hint: Excess.

Answer: A rise in the lake level flooded the dock by two inches. It looked like she was running on top of the water, but actually she was running on top of the dock.

31. The Document

Hint: Governmental document.

Answer: CONSTITUTION.

32. The Walking Stick

Hint: Protection.

Answer: He does this to deter snakes in his path. The snakes feel the vibrations from the pounding and slither away.

33. Dimes and Cups

Hint: There is no empty cup. Think what you can do with the third cup.

Answer: Yes, this can be done. Put five dimes in one cup. Put three dimes in another cup. Now choose <u>one</u> of these two cups and place it inside of the third cup.

34. Strange Rescuer

Hint: Most excellent friend.

Answer: He was rescued by a dog.

35. One Die

Hint: Less than six.

Answer: The probability is 5/36 or 13.89%; 1+5 / 2+4 / 3+3 / 4+2 / 5+1

36. Lights During the Day

Hint: An astronomical event.

Answer: There was a solar eclipse. The lights came on for a short time because they are equipped with photocell sensors that activate in low light conditions.

37. Unscramble

Hint: Flowers.

Answer: The 8-letter word is daffodil and the 4-letter word is rose.

38. Mount Rushmore

Hint: 16th president.

Answer: Abraham Lincoln. He represents the ideas of equality and a permanent union of states.

39. Rearrange the Tiles

Hint: Paul Revere.

Answer: "The British are coming."

Note: Although this has been attributed to Paul Revere, some historians argue the accuracy of this quote.

40. A Long Way Home

Hint: Relay.

Answer: There were 20 volunteer drivers strategically located along the route. Each driver transported the dog for approximately 100 miles of the trip.

41. Mental Division 2

Hints: 1. Whole number. 2. Mixed numeral.

Answers:

1. 16.

2. 3 and 1/5 or 3.2.

42. Several Operators

Hint: Relay.

Answers: It was the Pony Express. They delivered the mail.

43. Not So Common Word

Hint: A cross between.

Answer: A zonkey is hybrid animal that is a cross between a female donkey and a male zebra. The zonkey is a sterile animal, which means it cannot reproduce. A zonkey is a donkey-like animal that often has zebra-like stripes.

44. Trapped by Fire

Hint: Something outside.

Answer: The couple survived by getting into their neighbor's outdoor pool as the fire burned all around.

45. Roman Numerals

Hint: More than 150 years ago.

Answers: The number is 1865. It is the year the Civil War in the United States ended.

46. Goats on a Dam Wall

Hint: A mineral compound found in your diet.

Answers:

1. The goats need for salt because their diet is salt-deficient. Without salt their nerves and muscles do not function properly.

2. Salt is especially import to the females when they are feeding their young.

47. Leslie's Goal

Hint: Green once.

Answer:

Leslie hikes these trails:

Red = 1.0 mi. 2 times
Yellow = 2.1 mi. 3 times
Blue = 6.0 mi. 1 time
Orange = 0.7 mi. 1 time
White = 2.0 mi. 1 time
Green = 3.0 mi. 1 time

48. Is There Water on the Moon?

Hint: Rime and ends.

Answers: Yes, as water ice. It is located at the poles.

49. Tennessee Road Trip

Hint: The car used is just a regular automobile, nothing special.

Answer: There is no missing hour. Chattanooga is on Eastern Standard Time (EST) while Franklin is on Central Standard Time (CST). It still took two hours.

50. Hard-Boiled Eggs

Hint: Higher.

Answer: At higher altitudes, water boils at a lower temperature, so boiled food needs to be cooked longer.

51. Fresh Water

Hint: Solar.

Answer: Put some ocean water into the large bowl. Place the cup in the center of the bowl making sure that the top of the cup is above the salt-water line. Lay the saran wrap over the bowl and securing it at the edges to make a good seal. Place a small pebble on top of the saran wrap in the center. Place this arrangement in the sun. The sun will cause water, but not the salt, to evaporate and collect on the bottom side of the saran wrap. It will move to the center and drop into the cup.

52. A Raisin

Hint: Begins with the letter "O."

Answer: Osmosis. The water isn't simply flowing into the raisin. It is passing through the cell walls of the raisin.

53. Long Distance Runner

Hint: Higher.

Answer: Physical performance decreases above 6,000 feet of elevation. The air has less oxygen, which causes shortness of breath as well as increased heart rate during exercise.

Note: Clingmans Dome has an elevation of 6,643 feet.

54. Turning Left

Hint: Sport.

Answers: The two men are the catcher and the umpire.

55. Partners

Hint: Map or globe.

Answers: We are longitude and latitude.

56. Two Oval Shapes

Hint: Reflection.

Answer: The light from the bathroom light hits the metal hinges casting an oval reflection onto the linen closet door. Only when the light is on and the bathroom door is open do the oval shapes appear.

57. How Many Package Deals?

Hint: Add, divide, and round.

Answer: He needs to sell 11 complete condo home packages.

58. Stay Alive

Hint: Temperature.

Answers: Your body will lose heat while eating the snow, which could lower your core body temperature. Melt the snow by a fire or by the heater inside of your car.

59. Eight Years

Hint: Leap year.

Answer: 2,922 = (8 x 365) + 2. Leap years occur in 2020 and 2024, with 366 days in each.

60. Hold Your Horses

Hint: Look.

Answer: Horses can remember facial expressions.

61. More Than 2,000 Miles

Hint: Path.

Answer: I am the Appalachian Trail.

62. Unusual Villages

Hint: Detached.

Answer: They are floating villages built on water.

63. Gasoline

Hint: Multiply and divide.

Answers: The cost is $32.13. The miles per gallon is 19.5.

64. Near the Continental Divide

Hint: Near Butte.

Answers: My name is Helena. I am the capital of Montana.

65. Six Questions

Hint: Multiply.

Answers:

1. 36 months.
2. 156 weeks and 3 days or 156 3/7 weeks.
3. 1,095 days.
4. 26,280 hours.
5. 1,576,800 minutes.
6. 94,608,000 seconds.

66. Improving Indoor Air Quality

Hint: Natural element.

Answer: A natural component would be selecting the best plants to absorb carbon dioxide while giving off oxygen.

Note: Here are a few plants that improve indoor air quality: Spider Plant, Peace Lily, Boston Fern, and Aloe Vera.

67. A Circle

Hint: Use $\pi = 3.14$

Answers:

Circumference = $2\pi r$ = 2 x 3.14 x 4 = 25.12 inches

Area = πr^2 = 3.14 x 16 = 50.24 sq. inches

68. Small, but Powerful

Hint: Moisture.

Answer: I am hail.

69. Bigger Than Two States

Hint: Park.

Answer: I am Yellowstone National Park.

70. Riptides

Hint: Parallel.

Answers:

1. He swam parallel to the shore, which freed himself from the riptide. Most riptides are less than 30 feet wide.
2. When he got tired he conserved his energy by floating on his back.
3. Once free, he swam diagonally toward the shore in order not to be pulled back into the riptide. And he avoided swimming near any jetties or structures as riptides can form by them.

71. Work for Free

Hint: Not like me or you.

Answer: I am a robot.

72. Window Shopping

Hint: Common machine.

Answer: A vacuum cleaner was attached under the garbage bags, creating a vacuum holding him in place on the outside of the storefront window.

73. No Train Engines

Hint: Secrets.

Answer: I am the Underground Railroad.

74. Methane Gas

Hint: Solids and gas.

Answers:

1. Cows are a major producer of methane on a farm.
2. The three forms are: manure, belching, and flatulence (least amount).

75. Coded Message 2

Hint: Our country's announcement.

Answer: The Declaration of Independence.

Note: This is a minus 1 alphabet code. Some examples are as follows:

$$A = 1 - 1 = 0$$
$$B = 2 - 1 = 1$$
$$C = 3 - 1 = 2$$

76. Find the Answer

Hint: You.

Answer: Your birthdate is the answer.

Chapter Six

ADVANCED
HINTS AND ANSWERS

77. Tiles

Hint: Experts.

Answer: SCIENTISTS

78. Tiger Attacks

Hint: Wearing something.

Answer: They wore masks on the back of their heads.

79. A Football

Hint: Codes. Presidential.

Answer: I am the President's nuclear codes.

80. Four-Wheeler

Hint: Fulcrum.

Answer: They cut down a small tree and another chunk of wood to make a fulcrum to lift the wheel. Then, they placed chunks of wood under the wheel until they got it level.

81. Container Ships

Hint: A marking.

Answer: They ensure that the water level does not go above the International Load Line, or Plimsoll Line, which is painted on the side at mid-ship. This line is identified by a circle symbol with a horizontal line running through it.

Note: There are six variations of this line depending on the different types of water such as salt, fresh, tropical, summertime, winter, and winter N. Atlantic.

82. Surviving an Avalanche

Hint: Preserve and pause.

Answers:

Step 3 - Save your air and your energy. You might be able to dig yourself out, if you are close to the top. If not, you are not going to get out by yourself. If you hear other people, call out to them, but don't overdo it.

Step 4 - Wait for rescuers to come. If you had an avalanche beacon with you, others will be able to find you. Stay calm.

83. Rainbow-Colored Lights

Hint: Ice crystals.

Answer: The nearly flat hexagon shaped ice crystals were reflecting the city lights. These ice crystals occur at higher level clouds when the temperature is very cold.

84. A Misunderstanding

Hint: Rain

Answer: He left his car lights on, which would have caused the battery to die by the end of the day. A good person disconnected his battery to prevent this from happening.

85. Adjusting a Spotlight

Hint: She used a homeowner's piece of equipment.

Answer: She laid an extension ladder across the slip opening and then placed several boards on it. This allowed her to walk onto the ladder to adjust the light.

86. I Created Many Things

Hint: Synthetic and blocks.

Answers:

> 1. I made wood shavings into synthetic marble.
> 2. I made cotton into paving blocks.

87. Safer Water

Hint: Seep.

Answer: He dug a seep (hole) next to the stream, thus filtering out many contaminates. This allowed the water to filter through the soil, which reduced his chances of getting sick. By digging a second hole a few inches away from the first hole allowed the water to seep from one hole into the second hole. This added more safety to drinking this water. While it is safer to drink water from a double seep than directly from a stream, this is not for certain. If possible, always boil your water to be safe.

88. Fifty States

Hint: Pleasant and travel.

Answers:

1. In 1986, it became the law to be nice. It is known as the "Aloha Spirit" law.
2. Hawaii depends on its nine million visitors each year. So, being nice makes sense.

89. No Keys

Hint: A severed isthmus.

Answer: I am the Panama Canal.

90. Setting A Record

Hint: Sound.

Answer: He was the first to break the sound barrier.

91. Cryogenic Freezing

Hint: Parasitic.

Answer: Nematode roundworms. They were placed in Petri dishes with nutrient jelly at 68 degrees F. After a few days, they began to move.

92. The Color of Snow

Hint: Warm climate.

Answer: Sand from sandstorms in the Sahara Desert in North Africa is sucked up into the atmosphere and mixes with precipitation, providing an orange hue to the snow. It reaches Russia by the normal western weather moving to the east.

93. We Made a Big Difference

Hint: Native.

Answer: We were the Navajo Code Talkers.

94. Getting Out of Quicksand

Hint: Park and turn.

Answers:

Step 3 - Sit down and lean back if your feet get stuck. This should help to free your feet. When you feel them become free, roll onto your side moving away from the quicksand pit.

Step 4 - Take your time and do things slowly. Slow movements work best in quicksand. It may take a while to get free.

95. A Dakota Fire Pit

Hint: Temperature and fuel.

Answer:

1. The fire burns very hot.
2. Less firewood is needed.
3. Less smoke is produced.

96. Paint Purchase

Hint: Compute the square footage to be painted in one apartment. Then subtract the 3-bedroom doors and 3-bedroom windows from the painted areas.

Answer: 27 gallons.

Bedroom one walls = 10 x 8 x 2 walls + 12 x 8 x 2 walls = 352 sq. ft.
Bedroom two walls = 12 x 8 x 2 walls + 14 x 8 x2 walls = 416 sq. ft.
Bedroom three walls = 14 x 8 x 2 walls + 16 x 8 x 2walls = 480 sq. ft.
Total 1248 sq. ft.
Less doors = 3 x 7 x 3 bedrooms = 63 sq. ft.
Less windows = 6 x 6 x 3 bedrooms = 108 sq. ft.
Total 1077 sq. ft.
x 10
Total square footage 10,770 sq. ft.
10,770 sq. ft. ÷ 400 sq. ft. per gallon = 26.925
Round up to 27 gallons

97. A Big Appetite

Hint: A depression.

Answer: I am a sinkhole.

98. The Bottle

Hint: Not heads up.

Answer: He dropped the nail head first into the bottle. By shaking it up and down and in a circular fashion, the nail made small cracks in the base of the bottle causing it to drop out.

99. Boiling River

Hint: What lies below?

Answer: Since the nearest volcano is more than 400 miles away, Dr. Andres Ruzo thinks the heat source is non-volcanic. He believes the heat source is a large hydro-thermo system underground.

100. Big Square

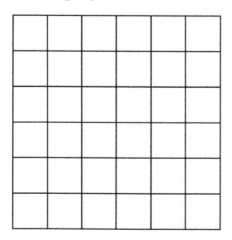

Hint: Some squares may overlap. There is an algorithm that makes this easier. If you figured out the answers to a 3x3 square and also a 4x4 square, then you might guess the algorithm that could apply to this 6x6 square.

Answer: There are 91 squares as follows:

(1) large 6x6 square + (36) singles squares + (25) 2x2 squares + (16) 3x3 squares + (9)4x4 squares + (4) 5x5 squares = 91 squares.

Note:

The algorithm for this square and others will be found in Volume 3 of CHALLENGE YOUR KIDS.

REFERENCES

1 Creative Commons. This Photo by Unknown Author is licensed under CC BY-SA
https://www.flickr.com/photos/53801255@N07/7095644699/

2 Tammi Marie. "How to put a person inside of a swimming bathing cap." Online video clip. YouTube. YouTube, 5 July 2010. Web 11 Dec. 2018.

3 Newsy Science. "Astronaut Scott Kelly is 2 Inches Taller Now Because SPACE." Online video clip. YouTube. YouTube, 3 Mar. 2016. Web 14 Dec. 2018.

4 WikiHow Contributors. "How to Calculate Multiple Dice Probabilities." WikiHow to do anything. WikiHow to do anything, Web 25 Aug. 2018. https://www.wikihow.com/Calculate-Multiple-Dice-Probabilities

5 National Park Service Contributors. "Synchronous Fireflies." National Park Service. National Park Service, Web 25 Aug. 2018. https://www.nps.gov/grsm/learn/nature/fireflies.htm

6 "Literary Terms." Literary Terms. 1 June 2015. Web. 9 Aug. 2018. https://literaryterms.net/rebus

7 Creative Commons. https://creativecommons.org/licenses/by-sa/3.0/ Bee. http://ielselog.blogspot.com/p/blogger_29.html. Oar. https://en.wikipedia.org/wiki/Paddle. Knot. https://puzzling.stackexchange.com/questions/55508/my-friends-rope-puzzle.

8 Ducksters Contributors. "Biography Rosa Parks." Ducksters Education Site. Ducksters Education Site, Web 14 Dec. 2018. https://www.ducksters.com/biography/women_leaders/rosa_parks.php

9 MSN Contributor. "Seagull Knocks on Window for Food Every Day." MSN Video. MSN Video 26 Oct. 2018. Web 1 Dec. 2018. https://www.msn.com/en-us/video/animals/seagull-knocks-on-window-for-food-every-day/vi-BBOZTp2

10 Anna P. "Dog Rescues Man Drowning in a River." Fuzzydose. Fuzzydose, Web 10 Dec. 2018. http://fuzzydose.com/dog-rescues-man-drowning-in-a-river/

11 National Park Contributors. "Why These Four Presidents?" National Park Service. National Park Service, Web 1 Nov. 2018. https://www.nps.gov/moru/learn/historyculture/why-these-four-presidents.htm

12 Feinn, Lily. "Dog Goes Missing from Home - And Turns Up 2,000 Miles Away." The Dodo. The Dodo, 24 May 2018. Web 2 June 2018. https://www.thedodo.com/close-to-home/lost-dog-traveled-2000-miles-returns-to-family

13 National Park Service Contributors. "Pony Express." National Park Service. National Park Service, Web 5 Aug. 2018. https://www.nps.gov/poex/learn/historyculture/index.htm

14 A-Z Animals Contributors. "Zonkey." A-Z Animals. A-Z Animals, Web 10 Aug. 2018. https://a-z-animals.com/animals/zonkey/

15 Abcarian. Robin. "They survived six hours in a pool as a wildfire burned their neighborhood to the ground." Los Angeles Times. 12 Oct. 2017. Web 19 Oct. 2018. https://www.latimes.com/local/abcarian/la-me-abcarian-sonoma-fire-20171012-htmlstory.html

16 Buzznick Contributors. "Look at These Gravity Defying Goats Climbing A Dam Wall." Buzznick. Buzznick, Web 20 Oct. 2018. https://www.buzznick.com/objects-on-dam/

17 Samaa TV Contributors. "Scientists Confirm Ice Exists at Moon's Poles." Samma TV. Samaa TV, 22 Aug. 2018. Web 26 Aug, 2018.

18 Wonderopolis Contributors. "Why Does Water Boil Faster at Higher Altitude?" Wonderopolis. Wonderopolis, Web 3 Jan. 2019.

19 Dallas, Mary Elizabeth. "Horses Can Read Human Facial Expressions." CBS News. CBS News, 11 Feb. 2016. Web 3 Jan. 2019. https://www.cbsnews.com/news/horses-can-read-human-facial-expressions/

20 Stacke, Sarah. "Immigrants Find Homes in Colorful Floating Villages." National Geographic. National Geographic, 3 Jan. 2018. Web 22 Apr. 2018. https://www.nationalgeographic.com/photography/proof/2018/01/cambodia-boat-homes-fedorenko/

21 Cell Press. "Using the right plants can reduce indoor pollution and save energy." ScienceDaily. ScienceDaily, 19 April 2018. Web 21 June 2018. www.sciencedaily.com/releases/2018/04/180419131121.htm.

22 Creative Commons. This Photo by Unknown Author is licensed under CC BY-SA https://ja.wikibooks.org/wiki/ファイル: Circle_and_radius.svg

23 WikiHow Staff. "How to Survive a Rip Tide." WikiHow. WikiHow, Web 20 Oct. 2018. https://www.wikihow.com/Survive-a-Rip-Tide

24 Outrageous Acts of Science. Year and Date Unknown.

25 Silverman, Jacob. "Do Cows Pollute as Much as Cars?" HowStuffWorks. HowStuffWorks, Web 21 July 2018. https://animals.howstuffworks.com/mammals/methane-cow.htm

26 Grasso, Lenox. "Deciphering Merchant Ship Hull Markings." American Sailing Association Nautical Trivia. American Sailing Association Nautical Trivia, 10 May 2018. Web 4 Jan. 2019. https://asa.com/news/2018/05/10/merchant-ship-hull-markings/

27 WikiHow Staff. "How to Survive an Avalanche." WikiHow. WikiHow, 18 Nov. 2006. Web. 2 Nov. 2018.

28 Earl, Jennifer. "The Rare Phenomenon That Lit Up Wyoming's Sky". CBS News. CBS News, Updated 5 Feb. 2017. Web 10 Oct. 2018. https://www.cbsnews.com/news/the-rare-phenomenon-that-lit-up-wyomings-sky-this-week/

29 Contributors. "George Washington Carver's Inventions." Intellectualvillage. Intellectualvillage, 12 July 2007. Web 29 June 2018. http://www.intellectualvillage.com/inventionspatents/george-washington-carvers-inventions/

30 Lawrence, Mark. "How to Find Water in the Wilderness." Secrets of Survival. Secrets of Survival. Web 2 Oct. 2018. https://www.secretsofsurvival.com/survival/How-to-Find-Water-in-the-Wilderness.html

31 Kerr, Breena. "In Hawaii, Being Nice Is the Law." BBC. BBC, 23 Apr. 2018. Web 1 Sept. 2018. http://www.bbc.com/travel/story/20180422-in-hawaii-being-nice-is-the-law

32 Waugh, Rob. "Is Cryogenic Freezing Possible? Worms Frozen For 40,000 Years Come Back to Life." Yahoo News UK. Yahoo News UK, 27 July 2018. Web 15 Aug. 2018. https://sg.news.yahoo.com/cryogenic-freezing-possible-worms-frozen-40000-years-come-back-life-121618624.html

33 Chen, Angela. "Here's Why the Snow in Russia Turned Orange." The Verge. The Verge, 26 Mar. 2018. Web 4 June 2018. https://www.theverge.com/2018/3/26/17165186/russia-snow-orange-dust-sahara-weather

34 Central Intelligence Agency Contributors. "Navajo Code Talkers and the Unbreakable Code." Central Intelligence Agency. Central Intelligence Agency, 2008 Archive. Web 5 Oct. 2018. https://www.cia.gov/news-information/featured-story-archive/2008-featured-story-archive/navajo-code-talkers/

35 WikiHow Staff. "How to Get Out of Quicksand." Wikihow. Wikihow, Web 11 Aug. 2018. https://www.wikihow.com/Get-out-of-Quicksand

36 Jorgustin, Ken. "Advantages of the Dakota Fire Hole - Smokeless Fire Pit." Modern Survival Blog. Modern Survival Blog, 30 Aug. 2018. Web 22 Sept. 2018. https://modernsurvivalblog.com/survival-skills/advantages-of-the-dakota-fire-hole/

37 Mb5n5377189. "Knocking the Bottom Out of a Beer Bottle." Online video clip. YouTube. YouTube, 24 May 2009. Web 3 Oct. 2018.

38 Ruzo, Andres. "The Boiling River of The Amazon." Ted Talk. Ted Talk, Oct. 2014. Web 15 Feb. 2019 https://www.bing.com/videos/search?q=ted+talk+andres+ruzo&view=detail&mid=41770FEB6F43A6DC473A41770FEB6F43A6DC473A&FORM=VIRE

ABOUT THE AUTHOR

DAVE VACCARO

For more than thirty years, I served as a teacher and a principal. In my classroom, I presented kids with problems I already knew and those I had created. I always did this in a group setting so they could solve problems together. At home and on road trips, I presented many of these same problems to my own kids, to my nieces and nephews, and now to my grandkids. I live in Tennessee with my wonderful wife Leslie.

A CUSTOMER REVIEW

I hope you enjoyed using these problems, brain teasers, and riddles with your kids. If so, please consider writing a short customer review on Amazon. This would help us reach more teachers, more parents, and more kids. You can do this by going to amazon.com and search for CHALLENGE YOUR KIDS, Volume 2, by Dave Vaccaro. Your help is appreciated.

THANK YOU

Thank you for purchasing this book. I hope this book helps you to challenge your kids in an enjoyable way. Visit our website for more problems, brain teasers, and riddles at www.challengeyourkidsnow.com.

Please share this book with your friends.

Made in the USA
Middletown, DE
14 February 2023

24878971R00056